# sandwiched

GRILL 'EM | TOAST 'EM | STUFF 'EM | EAT 'EM

# praise for *sandwiched*

*"Move over, peanut butter and jam! Tanya's creative and delicious gourmet sandwich recipes in* Sandwiched: Grill 'Em, Toast 'Em, Stuff 'Em, Eat 'Em *are absolutely drool-worthy! From savory Greek Meatball Sliders to delectable Caramel Apple French Toast, there is something for everyone in this book. You will never look at two pieces of bread in the same way again!"*

—Camille Beckstrand, author and blogger at SixSistersStuff.com

*"Sandwich lovers rejoice! I've been an avid follower of Tanya's blog, Lemons for Lulu, for a long time, and I love her easy twists on preparing fresh, simple food for your family. With Tanya's book,* Sandwiched, *you'll never go back to boring turkey and cheese sandwiches again. Filled with tasty, mouth-watering recipes like Vegetarian Bánh Mì, Chocolate Peanut Butter Sandwich Cookies, and Chicken Parmesan Sliders, there is something here for everyone to enjoy. If you're looking for fun new ways to jazz up plain-jane sandwiches, you need to get your hands on this book!"*

—Ashley Whitmore, founder and author of KitchenMeetsGirl.com

*"I am somewhat of a rebel when it comes to food. I've been known to serve french toast for dinner or BLT for breakfast. I also believe that sandwiches should be enjoyed ANY time of the day! No, they are not just for lunch. With her new book,* Sandwiched: Grill 'Em, Toast 'Em, Stuff 'Em, Eat 'Em, *Tanya Schroeder will help you enjoy creative sandwiches any time of the day. Whether you want one for breakfast, dinner, or dessert, she has a perfect recipe to keep you satisfied."*

—Lyuba Brooke, author of *The Pumpkin Lover's Cookbook* and willcookforsmiles.com

# sandwiched

GRILL 'EM | TOAST 'EM | STUFF 'EM | EAT 'EM

TANYA SCHROEDER

FRONT TABLE BOOKS
AN IMPRINT OF CEDAR FORT, INC. | SPRINGVILLE, UTAH

ISBN 13: 978-1-4621-1697-3

Published by Front Table Books, an imprint of Cedar Fort, Inc.
2373 W. 700 S., Springville, UT 84663
Distributed by Cedar Fort, Inc., www.cedarfort.com

LIBRARY OF CONGRESS CATALOGING-IN-PUBLICATION DATA

Schroeder, Tanya, 1972-
Sandwiched / Tanya Schroeder.
pages cm
Includes index.
ISBN 978-1-4621-1697-3 (hardback : acid-free paper)
1. Sandwiches. I. Title.
TX818.S37 2015
641.84--dc23
2015017936

Cover design by M. Shaun McMurdie and Michelle May
Page design by Michelle May
Cover design © 2015 by Lyle Mortimer
Edited by Justin Greer

Printed in the United States of America

10 9 8 7 6 5 4 3 2 1

Printed on acid-free paper

# contents

# introduction

Why a sandwich book? I have eaten over 4,764,295 turkey sandwiches in my lifetime. Okay, okay, that might a slight exaggeration. But I've definitely overdosed on turkey . . . and peanut butter . . . and ham . . . and salami. One can only consume so many turkey sandwiches!

Sandwiches are easy and fun, and they come in an enormous variety of sizes, shapes, and flavors. You can grill them, toast them, and stuff them. They can range from the simple to the sublime; the sky is truly the limit!

My goal for this book is to introduce you to a few new ways to enjoy sandwiches that go beyond the deli case. In this book you will find hot and cold sandwiches, quick and easy sandwiches, and sandwiches that may take a bit of planning. You will find two-bite party sandwiches, breakfast sandwiches, main meal sandwiches, and even sandwiches that will satisfy your sweet tooth. The one thing that is consistent throughout this book is that all the recipes are simple, with ingredients readily found in your local supermarket. Let's face it, if a recipe has too many steps and too many fancy ingredients, the food isn't going to happen!

I wanted to keep the recipes in this book real, fun, and simple. I hope I've accomplished that.

I have fallen in love with so many sandwiches in this book! My personal favorites are the Vegetarian Bánh Mì; the Parmesan Sliders; and the Fig, Brie, and Caramelized Onion Grilled Cheese. My family declared the Mocha Donut sandwich, the Caramel Apple French Toast, the Smoked Salmon, and the Crab Cakes to be the best. I would love to know which sandwiches *you* love!

Grab some bread and let's make some sandwiches!

# starter sammies

***"Hors-d'oeuvre: A ham sandwich cut into forty pieces."***
***—Jack Benny***

# chicken parmesan sliders

*Every year, I make chicken parmesan for my husband's birthday. This sandwich is my tribute to him! These sandwiches are perfect for parties that require a little more than chips and dip!*

Prep time: 10 minutes | Cook time: 18 minutes | Makes: 12 sandwiches

### CHICKEN SLIDERS

2 lb. ground chicken
1 teaspoon dried basil
1 teaspoon dried oregano
½ teaspoon dried thyme
½ teaspoon garlic powder
2 tablespoons fresh parsley
¼ cup grated Parmesan cheese
½ cup Italian-style bread crumbs
12 slices fresh mozzarella cheese

### SAUCE

1 teaspoon olive oil
2 cloves garlic, minced
½ red pepper flakes
½ teaspoon dried basil
14 oz. crushed tomatoes
2 tablespoons tomato paste
¼ teaspoon salt
2 tablespoon fresh basil finely chopped

12 whole wheat slider rolls

Preheat oven to 400 degrees.

In a bowl, combine chicken, herbs, parsley, Parmesan cheese, and bread crumbs. Mix by hand until blended. Shape chicken mixture into 12 patties. Place on lightly greased baking sheet. Bake for 15 minutes, turning once. Top each slider with mozzarella slice. Bake an additional 3 minutes or until cheese is bubbly and melted.

Meanwhile, heat saucepan over medium heat. Heat oil, add garlic, and cook for 1 minute. Stir in pepper flakes and dried basil. Heat an additional minute. Reduce heat and stir in crushed tomatoes and tomato paste. Add salt. Continue to heat on low until warm.

When sliders are ready and cheese has melted, place one slider on each roll. Divide sauce among each slider. Sprinkle basil over sliders just before serving.

# smoked salmon finger sandwiches

*Smoked salmon and horseradish are a match made in heaven in these easy finger sandwiches.*

Prep time: 10 minutes | Makes: 16 sandwiches

- 4 oz. cream cheese, softened
- 1 tablespoon milk
- 1 tablespoon prepared horseradish
- 12 oz. rye cocktail bread
- 4 oz. smoked salmon, sliced
- 1 teaspoon chopped chive
- pinch of salt and pepper
- 4–5 chives cut into 3-inch slices for garnish

In a bowl, combine cream cheese, milk, and horseradish until smooth.

Spread a generous spoonful of the cream cheese mixture on the bottoms of 8 pieces of bread. Top with a slice of smoked salmon, chives, and remaining bread.

Season with salt and pepper to taste. Add sliced chives for garnish.

# mini california club sandwiches

*Club sandwiches have something for everyone, especially with cool tomatoes and salty bacon. These mini sandwiches have creamy avocados too!*

Prep time: 15 minutes | Makes: 22 sandwiches

½ cup mayo
2 cloves garlic, minced
2 tablespoons Parmesan cheese
pepper to taste
1 lb. mini rye bread loaf
2 cups loosely packed baby kale
½ lb. deli turkey
4–5 roma tomatoes, sliced
10 strips of cooked bacon, broken into pieces
2 avocados, thinly sliced

In a small bowl, mix together mayo, garlic, and Parmesan cheese. Add pepper to taste.

Spread about a ½ teaspoon of mayo mixture on each slice of bread. Divide kale over mayo mixture. Place one slice of deli turkey over kale and top with tomato, bacon pieces, and avocado slices.

# cherry barbecue turkey sandwiches

*I'm a huge fan of spicy and sweet combinations. The sauce for these sliders is the perfect blend of both. The onion straws add crunch, while the buttermilk ranch is creamy and cool.*

**Prep time: 20 minutes | Cook time: 2 hours 10 minutes | Makes: 12 sandwiches**

TURKEY

1 tablespoon olive oil
2 cloves garlic, chopped
1 small shallot, diced
½ cup ketchup
¼ cup cherry preserves
¼ cup brown sugar
2 tablespoons apple cider vinegar
¼ teaspoon salt
½ teaspoon ancho chile powder
½ teaspoon cumin
1 (20-oz.) package turkey tenderloins

ONION STRAWS

2 cups flour
4 teaspoons salt
2 teaspoons pepper
2 large onions, sliced into rings
1½ cups vegetable oil

RANCH SAUCE:

2 tablespoons plain Greek yogurt
4 tablespoons buttermilk
1 tablespoon ranch seasoning mix

12 mini sandwich rolls

To prepare the cherry barbecue sauce, combine olive oil, garlic, and shallots in a small saucepan. Cook over medium-low heat until shallots begin to soften, about 2–3 minutes. Stir in ketchup, cherry preserves, and remaining ingredients (through cumin). Reduce heat to low, and continue to stir. Cook until sauce begins to thicken, about 20 minutes.

Place turkey in a slow cooker. Pour sauce over turkey. Cover and cook on high for 2 hours. Remove turkey and shred with two forks. Place shredded turkey back into slow cooker, turning to coat each piece with the cherry sauce. Keep warm.

To prepare the straws, combine flour, salt, and pepper in a large ziplock back. Add onions and toss to coat each piece.

Heat oil in a large, deep pan until oil reaches 365 degrees. Add onions and fry just until they are golden, 3–4 minutes. Be sure to only add a few onion straws at a time, taking care not to crowd your pan. Remove onions and place on a baking sheet lined with a paper towel. Repeat with any remaining onions.

For the ranch sauce, combine yogurt, ranch seasoning, and buttermilk in a bowl.

Divide turkey and onions among each sandwich roll. Drizzle buttermilk sauce over onions. Serve.

# greek meatball sliders

*Who doesn't love a good meatball? These juicy sliders pay homage to my Greek heritage.* Opa! *That's all I have to say.*

Prep time: 10 minutes | Cook time: 22 minutes | Makes: 12 sandwiches

MEATBALLS

1 teaspoon olive oil
¼ cup chopped onions
1 clove garlic, minced
2 slices of white bread, crusts removed
¼ cup milk
1 lb. lean ground beef
1 teaspoon dried oregano
½ teaspoon dried thyme
½ teaspoon salt
1 egg, lightly beaten

TZATZIKI SAUCE

4 tablespoons plain Greek yogurt
1 tablespoon lemon juice
2 teaspoons finely grated, peeled, seedless cucumber
1 clove garlic, minced
½ teaspoon garlic

TOPPINGS

1 cup loosely packed spinach leaves
¼ cup sliced red onions
3 oz. crumbled feta cheese
12 roma tomatoes, sliced
⅓ cup sliced, pitted black olives

12 slider buns

Preheat oven to 425 degrees.

Heat olive oil in a small skillet over medium heat. Add onions and garlic, and cook until onions have softened and become translucent, about 5 minutes. Remove from heat and let cool.

Place bread in a small bowl and cover with milk.

In a large bowl, combine ground beef, oregano, thyme, and salt. Add egg. Squeeze milk from bread slices with your hand and add to ground beef mixture. Add cooled onions and garlic as well. Mix beef by hand until egg and bread have been incorporated.

Using a small cookie scoop or your hands, shape meat mixture into 12 equal pieces. Try to get all 12 meatballs as uniform as possible.

Place meatballs on a baking sheet coated with cooking spray. Bake for 18–22 minutes. Remove meatballs from oven and let cool.

To prepare the sauce, combine all the ingredients in a bowl; stir.

To assemble sliders, divide spinach equally among the bottoms of 12 slider buns, along with red onions and ½ tablespoon of feta. Place one meatball over feta cheese. Drizzle tzatziki sauce over each slider. Top each slider with one slice of tomato and a teaspoon of olives. Serve.

# mini caprese sandwiches

*Caprese salads have always been my favorite. There is something about the combination of fresh basil, crisp tomatoes, and creamy mozzarella that makes me melt! This is my sandwich version of that irresistible salad!*

Prep time: 10 minutes | Makes: 12 Sandwiches

½ cup olive oil
4 cloves garlic
12 butter dinner rolls
½ cup loosely packed fresh basil leaves
1 lb. fresh mozzarella cheese, sliced into 12 equal portions
4 medium sized vine-ripened tomatoes
1 teaspoon salt

Heat oil in a small saucepan over medium heat. Add garlic and heat until garlic begins to sizzle.

Cut rolls in half. Brush garlic oil generously over each bun half. Place a few leaves of basil over each bottom bun. Top basil with mozzarella and one tomato slice. Sprinkle tomato slices with salt and top with remaining bun.

# bacon, cheddar, ranch pimento cheese party sandwiches

*Sometimes I think I'm a Southern girl at heart. I could eat this pimento cheese with a spoon!*

Prep time: 15 minutes | Makes: 22 sandwiches

- 1 cup pepper jack cheese, grated
- 1 cup white cheddar cheese, grated
- 1 cup Monterey Jack cheese, grated
- 1 (4-oz) jar pimentos, drained
- 1 cup mayo
- 1 tablespoon ranch seasoning
- 3 slices cooked bacon, chopped
- 1 lb. pumpernickel mini bread loaf

Combine pepper jack cheese, white cheddar cheese, Monterey Jack cheese, pimentos, mayo, ranch seasoning, and bacon in a large bowl. Mix until completely combined. Divide pimento cheese among bread slices, and serve.

# breakfast sammies

***Hans: We finish each other's—***
***Anna: Sandwiches!***
***Hans: That's what I was going to say!***
**—Frozen**

# chicken biscuit sandwich with mushroom gravy

*This is my take on two classics: biscuits and gravy and chicken fried steak!*

Prep time: 5 minutes | Cook time: 30 minutes | Makes: 8 sandwiches

1 (16.3-oz) can buttermilk biscuits

CHICKEN

oil
1 cup buttermilk
dash of hot sauce (optional)
2 cups self-rising flour
1 teaspoon paprika
1 teaspoon oregano
½ teaspoon dried sage
1 teaspoon salt
1½ lb. chicken tenders

GRAVY

3 tablespoons butter
8 oz. chopped mushrooms
3 tablespoons flour
¾ teaspoon salt
¼ teaspoon pepper
½ teaspoon crushed red pepper
1 cup milk

Prepare biscuits according to package directions.

In a deep skillet, add oil up to an inch deep over medium heat.

Place buttermilk in a deep bowl.

Combine flour and seasoning in another bowl. Dredge chicken tenders in buttermilk, then dip in flour mixture. Coat chicken thoroughly, shaking off any excess flour.

Carefully place chicken in hot oil. Working in batches, fry chicken about 3 minutes per side or until golden in color. Remove chicken and drain on a paper towel-lined baking sheet. Keep chicken warm while you prepare the gravy.

Melt 3 tablespoons of butter in a large skillet. Add mushrooms and cook until soft (about 2 minutes). Whisk in flour. Slowly add milk and cook an additional 2 minutes or until gravy is thick. Add pepper and red pepper.

To assemble, slice each biscuit in half. Place chicken on bottom biscuit, ladle a spoonful of gravy over chicken, and top with second biscuit half.

Tip: An easy way to see if your oil is hot enough for frying is to place the handle of a wooden spoon in your oil. If the oil begins to bubble around the spoon, then your oil is the right temperature.

# sweet and savory poached egg sandwich

*Everything that makes breakfast the best meal of the day in one easy sandwich!*

Prep time: 5 minutes | Cook time: 20 minutes | Makes: 4 sandwiches

- 1 lb. turkey breakfast sausage, shaped into 4 patties
- 2 tablespoons of vinegar
- 4 eggs
- 2 teaspoons butter
- 4 English muffins, toasted
- 1 cup loosely packed spinach
- 4 slices white cheddar cheese
- 4 tablespoons apricot jam
- black pepper
- pinch of salt

Warm a griddle pan over medium heat. Add breakfast sausage and cook until fully browned on each side (about 6–8 minutes per side). Remove to a paper towel to drain.

To poach your eggs, fill a large, deep skillet with 2 inches of water. Add a pinch of salt to the water. Bring to a slow boil. When water begins to bubble, add two tablespoons of vinegar. When water comes to a gentle rolling boil, reduce heat. Crack each egg into a teacup or a ramekin. When water is ready, carefully drop cracked whole eggs into hot water. Eggs will start to set immediately. Cook eggs in water for 3 minutes. When ready, remove with a slotted spoon, draining all excess water.

To assemble, place a half teaspoon of butter on each muffin half. Top with ¼ cup spinach, cheese, tablespoon of jam, and a slice of hot sausage over jam. Arrange one poached egg over sausage. Sprinkle with pepper if desired. Serve immediately.

# caramel apple french toast

*Bring a little county fair into your breakfast with this French toast! The chopped hazelnuts add a sophisticated finish!*

Prep time: 10 minutes | Cook time: 8 minutes | Makes: 4 sandwiches

APPLES

1 tablespoon butter
1 green apple, finely diced
⅛ teaspoon cinnamon
1 tablespoon brown sugar

FRENCH TOAST

1 loaf French bread
5 eggs
2 cups of milk
½ teaspoon vanilla

CARAMEL SAUCE

½ cup butter
1 cup brown sugar
½ teaspoon vanilla

1 cup chopped, toasted hazelnuts

Slice bread into 12 slices that are each about 2 inches thick. Cut each slice in the middle, taking care not to cut straight through. You want to make a little pocket in each slice.

In a small skillet, melt 1 tablespoon of butter over low heat. Add apples, cinnamon, and brown sugar to skillet. Cook apples until slightly tender—this should take 3–5 minutes. Remove from heat and let apples cool. When apples are ready, spoon a tablespoon of apples into each French toast pocket.

In a bowl, whisk together eggs, milk, and vanilla. Heat a grill pan sprayed with nonstick spray over medium heat. Dunk each filled bread slice into egg mixture, turning to coat. Place bread on grill pan.

Toast each French toast slice for 2–4 minutes or until lightly toasted. Turn over and heat the second side for an additional 2–4 minutes. Remove and keep warm. Continue with remaining sandwiches, working in batches if necessary.

In a small saucepan, melt ½ cup butter over medium heat. Stir in brown sugar until well blended. Continue to cook an additional 5 minutes, or until thick. Remove from heat and stir in vanilla.

Serve each slice of French toast with toasted hazelnuts and caramel sauce.

# bourbon banana waffle sandwiches

*This is my sandwich take on a Bananas Foster dessert. Bourbon and thick Belgian waffles truly make this a decadent breakfast!*

Prep time: 5 minutes | Cook time: 15 minutes | Makes: 4 sandwiches

- 8 oz. cream cheese, softened
- ⅓ cup powdered sugar
- 2 teaspoons bourbon
- 1 tablespoon butter
- 2 sliced bananas
- ⅛ teaspoon cinnamon
- 4 teaspoons butter
- 8 Belgian waffles
- 8 teaspoons granola cereal
- maple syrup and powdered sugar to garnish

In a bowl, combine cream cheese, powdered sugar, and bourbon. Mix until combined and creamy.

Heat a small skillet over low heat and melt 1 tablespoon of butter. Add sliced banana and cinnamon. Sauté bananas 2–3 minutes, or until they soften. Remove from heat and set aside.

Heat a griddle pan over medium heat. Spread ½ teaspoon of butter over one side of each waffle. Place 4 waffles buttered side down on hot grill pan. Place a quarter of the cream mixture on each waffle. Divide bananas evenly over cream mixture, followed by 2 teaspoons of granola. Place remaining 4 waffles on top, buttered side up. Toast for 3–4 minutes or until golden, and carefully flip waffles over. Toast the second side for another 3–4 minutes, or until golden brown.

Serve with maple syrup.

# spicy eggs in purgatory sandwich

*Harissa is a fiery Middle Eastern pepper spread. Look for it in the ethnic section of your supermarket. Red pepper flakes or dried cayenne pepper can be substituted. Add spices to your taste.*

Prep time: 5 minutes | Cook time: 5 minutes | Makes: 4 sandwiches

TOMATO SAUCE

1 teaspoon olive oil
2 cloves garlic minced
1 (14-oz.) can crushed tomatoes
¼ teaspoon ground thyme
½ teaspoon dried oregano
½ teaspoon paprika
½ cup spicy Harissa
¾ teaspoon salt
pinch of sugar

SANDWICHES

4 eggs
4 bakery sandwich rolls
1 cup spinach
4 tablespoons feta cheese

Heat olive oil in a large skillet over medium heat. Add garlic and sauté for 1 minute. Stir in crushed tomatoes, thyme, oregano, paprika, Harissa, salt, and a pinch of sugar. Reduce heat and simmer on low while you prepare the eggs.

Spray a separate skillet over medium heat. Break eggs into the prepared skillet. Cook eggs until whites begin to set. This should take 1–2 minutes. Flip eggs and heat the second side for at least one minute, or until desired degree of doneness.

Place ¼ cup spinach on each of the bottoms of 4 rolls. Top spinach with ⅓ cup tomato mixture, one egg, and feta cheese. Place remaining roll on top. Serve.

# huevos rancheros breakfast quesadilla

*Move over, oatmeal; breakfast is about to become a fiesta!*

Prep time: 5 minutes | Cook time: 6 minutes | Makes: 4 quesadillas

1 (8.8-oz.) pkg. quick cooking Spanish rice, cooked
1 cup black beans, rinsed and drained
¼ cup salsa
4 eggs
4 (10-in.) tortillas
½ cup Monterey Jack cheese
salsa, avocados, sour cream, and jalapeños for garnish

In a bowl, combine rice, beans, and salsa.

Spray a skillet with nonstick spray and heat over medium heat. Add eggs and cook for 1–2 minutes or until the egg whites have set. Flip eggs and cook an additional minute, as if you were making your eggs over easy. Remove from heat and keep warm.

Spray skillet with nonstick spray. Add 1 tortilla. Place one tablespoon of cheese over one half of tortilla. Add ¼ of the rice mixture, followed by egg. Fold other half of tortilla over egg. Heat tortilla for 1–2 minutes, or until golden. Carefully flip over quesadilla and heat second side for an additional minute.

Repeat with remaining tortillas, cheese, rice, and eggs. Serve quesadillas with sour cream, avocados, and additional salsa, if desired.

# fork and knife breakfast hash sandwich

*These sandwiches have everything a good hash has and more! The creamy and cool avocado is the perfect way to tame the spicy chorizo and kick up the jack cheese!*

Prep time: 5 minutes | Cook time: 40 minutes | Makes: 4 sandwiches

2 teaspoons olive oil
½ cup russet potato, cubed
pinch of salt and pepper
1 lb. ground chorizo, divided and shaped into 4 equal patties
1 teaspoon butter
4 eggs
4 leaves of bibb lettuce
4 kaiser rolls, halved and toasted
4 slices pepper jack cheese
1 avocado, smashed

Heat oil in a medium skillet over medium-low heat. Add potatoes with a pinch of salt and pepper and brown them for 10–15 minutes. Remove and keep warm.

Shape your chorizo into 4 equal patties. Add chorizo patties to the same skillet and cook for 6–8 minutes per side. When patties are cooked through, remove them to a towel to drain. Keep chorizo warm.

Drain grease from your skillet and wipe pan.

Heat butter in skillet. Add eggs to the skillet. Cook on one side for 2 minutes or until egg whites are set. Flip and cook the second side for one minute.

Place lettuce on bottoms of each roll. Top lettuce with chorizo patties and place cheese on warm chorizo. Divide potatoes evenly over patties and top potatoes with fried egg. Spread a tablespoon of mashed avocado on each top roll. Place top roll avocado-side down onto potatoes.

# greek egg white omelet sandwich

*I never understood what the fuss was over egg white omelets. Then I tried one, and I became hooked!*

Prep time: 5 minutes | Cook time: 10 minutes | Makes: 2 sandwiches

½ teaspoon olive oil
¼ cup diced bell peppers
4 egg whites
2 tablespoons crumbled feta cheese
salt and pepper to taste
2 English muffins, toasted
½ cup loosely packed spinach
2 tablespoons black olives
2 tablespoons oil-packed sun-dried tomatoes

Heat oil in a small skillet and add bell pepper. Sauté until tender (3–4 minutes). Remove from heat and set aside.

Place the same skillet back on the heat. Add egg whites to pan. Tilt pan to allow egg whites to swirl and coat the entire pan. Place one tablespoon of feta cheese on the half of the omelet, opposite the handle. Lift handle of pan and gently slide top of the omelet over the half with the cheese. Sprinkle omelet with a pinch of salt and pepper and cook an additional 30 seconds. Remove to a cutting board. Cut omelet in half.

Top half of each muffin with a quarter cup of spinach, omelet half, and two tablespoons of peppers. Divide the olives and sun-dried tomatoes between both sandwiches. Sprinkle more feta cheese just before serving.

# main meal sammies

***"Many's the long night I've dreamed of cheese—toasted, mostly."***
***—Robert Louis Stevenson***

# cincinnati chili sloppy joe

*This recipe is inspired by my hometown. Cincinnati chili is a staple!*

Prep time: 5 minutes | Cook time: 15 minutes | Makes: 4 sandwiches

- 1 lb. lean ground beef
- ½ cup chopped onions
- 1 clove garlic, minced
- 1 cup tomato sauce
- 1 tablespoon apple cider vinegar
- 1 tablespoon Worcestershire sauce
- ¼ teaspoon cocoa powder
- ½ teaspoon salt
- 1 tablespoon chili powder
- 1 teaspoon cumin
- ¼ teaspoon cinnamon
- 1 teaspoon paprika
- ⅛ teaspoon cloves
- 1 (15-oz.) can chili beans, drained
- 4 hamburger buns
- shredded cheddar cheese

Heat a large skillet over medium heat. Add ground beef, onions, and garlic. Stir and crumble ground beef into small pieces. When beef is cooked through, stir in tomato sauce, vinegar, Worcestershire sauce, cocoa powder, salt, chili powder, cumin, cinnamon, paprika, cloves, and chili beans. Reduce heat to low and cook an additional 10 minutes, or until chili has thickened.

Spoon chili over the bottoms of your hamburger buns and top with cheese.

# caesar chicken salad sandwich

*Caesar is not just for salad! The flavor lends itself perfectly to this easy chicken sandwich.*

Prep time: 10 minutes | Makes: 4 sandwiches

4 tablespoons mayo
3 tablespoons water
3 tablespoons lemon juice
1 teaspoon Worcestershire sauce
¼ teaspoon salt
2 cups chopped cooked chicken
1 cup yellow cherry tomatoes, halved
2 tablespoons chopped red onion
2 tablespoons sunflower seeds
4 large croissants, halved
4 romaine lettuce leaves
½ cup shaved Parmigiano-Reggiano

In a bowl, combine mayonnaise, water, lemon juice, Worcestershire sauce, and salt. Stir in chicken, tomatoes, onion, and sunflower seeds, turning to coat.

Top the bottom half of each croissant with one leaf of lettuce. Divide salad among each croissant and top with shaved Parmesan cheese and remaining croissant half.

# pesto veggie sub

*The two foods I could live on are pesto and goat cheese. I could literally eat them with a spoon. In this case, with veggies!*

Prep time: 10 minutes | Cook time: 17 minutes | Makes: 4 sandwiches

1 zucchini sliced into ½-inch slices
1 squash, sliced
½ red onion, sliced
1 lb. sliced portobello mushrooms
1 cup prepared pesto
4 sub rolls, sliced
1 tablespoon mayo
4 oz. softened goat cheese
ground pepper

Preheat a grill pan. Place vegetables on pan and heat for 10–12 minutes or until veggies begin to soften. Remove veggies and place them in a bowl. Toss veggies with pesto.

While pan is still hot, toast bread slices cut side down for 5 minutes.

Spread mayonnaise on sub roll halves. Arrange veggies over sub rolls. Top veggies with crumbled goat cheese. Sprinkle pepper over sandwiches to taste.

# mediterranean chicken wrap

*Diving into my Mediterranean roots once more for this flavorful chicken wrap!*

Prep time: 5 minutes | Cook time: 8 minutes | Makes: 4 wraps

1 tablespoon olive oil

CHICKEN

3 lb. chicken tenders
1 teaspoon salt
1 teaspoon dried Greek seasoning

FILLING

1 cup hummus
1 cup mixed greens
½ cup sliced red onions
½ cucumber, sliced and halved
¼ cup sliced pepperoncini peppers
¼ cup crumbled feta cheese
4 whole wheat sandwich wraps

Heat a skillet with olive oil over medium heat. Sprinkle chicken with salt and Greek seasoning and add to hot skillet. Cook tenders for 6–8 minutes.

Spread ¼ cup of hummus over each wrap. Top each wrap with ¼ cup mixed greens. Slice chicken tenders and divide chicken equally and place over the greens in each wrap.

Top wraps with red onions, cucumber, pepperoncini peppers, and feta. Roll each wrap and cut in half before serving.

# fig, fontina, and caramelized onion grilled cheese

*Sweet onions and tangy figs complement one another perfectly in this easy grilled sandwich!*

Prep Time: 15 minutes | Cook Time: 6 minutes | Makes: 4 sandwiches

1 teaspoon olive oil
1 whole onion thinly sliced
4 teaspoons butter
8 slices ciabatta bread
4 slices fontina cheese
8 teaspoons fig jam

To caramelize the onions, heat olive oil in a large skillet over medium low heat. Add sliced onions. Cook on low heat for 12–15 minutes, or until onions have softened and turned caramel in color. Remove from heat.

Heat a grill pan over medium-low heat. Spread ½ teaspoon butter over each piece of bread, then place bread butter-side down onto hot grill pan to toast. Top each bread slice with a slice of fontina cheese, 2 tablespoons of onions, and 2 teaspoons of fig jam. Top each sandwich with remaining bread, buttered side up. Heat sandwiches for 2–3 minutes per side, or until gently toasted.

# chimichurri steak quesadilla

*Chimichurri is a green sauce that pairs well with grilled meat. It is the perfect condiment for steak quesadillas!*

Prep time: 5 minutes | Cook time: 25 minutes | Makes: 4 quesadillas

1 teaspoon olive oil
1½ lb. skirt steak
1 teaspoon salt
1 teaspoon pepper
1 teaspoon cumin
1 teaspoon oregano

CHIMICHURRI

½ cup loosely packed cilantro
½ cup loosely packed parsley
2 cloves garlic
¼ cup olive oil
1 tablespoon red wine vinegar
½ teaspoon salt

4 (10-inch) flour tortillas
4 tablespoons queso fresco

Heat olive oil in a skillet over medium heat. Season steak with salt, pepper, cumin, and oregano, then cut into strips. Cook steak until browned (2–3 minutes per side). Remove steak and wipe skillet with a paper towel.

Meanwhile, prepare the chimichurri by placing the remaining ingredients (cilantro through ½ teaspoon of salt) into a food processor. Process until mixture is combined.

To assemble, spray the same skillet with nonstick spray. Lay 1 tortilla on the skillet. Arrange steak slices over one half of the tortilla. Top steak with a spoonful of chimichurri over steak and sprinkle with 1 tablespoon of queso fresco. Fold tortilla over the steak and cook until underside is golden. Carefully flip tortilla over and brown the second side. Remove and repeat process with remaining tortillas and other ingredients. Cut each tortilla into wedges and serve.

# dilly tuna salad sandwich

*This is not your ordinary tuna salad! It's so fresh and flavorful. It will beat anything you find at a sub shop!*

Prep time: 5 minutes | Makes: 4 sandwiches

- 1 (12-oz.) can chunked tuna, packed in water
- 2 tablespoons Greek yogurt
- 2 tablespoons mayonnaise
- 2 tablespoons chopped fresh dill
- ¼ cup finely chopped cucumber
- 1 tablespoon chopped green onion
- ½ teaspoon lemon zest
- ¼ teaspoon salt
- 4 leaves of lettuce
- 2 tomatoes, sliced
- 8 slices of white bread

In a bowl, combine tuna, yogurt, mayonnaise, fresh dill, cucumber, green onion, lemon zest, and salt. Stir to combine.

Divide tuna, lettuce, and tomatoes between bread slices, and serve.

# toasted pizza sub

*My husband's hometown had the best pizza shop. Their pizza subs were simple but mighty addicting. This is my version of that sub.*

Prep time: 5 minutes | Cook time: 10 minutes | Makes: 4 sandwiches

4 hoagie rolls
2 teaspoons olive oil
1 clove garlic
3 Italian sausage links
8 oz. mushrooms
½ pound deli turkey
½ pound deli ham
½ pound Genoa salami
8 slices provolone cheese
½ cup prepared marinara sauce

Preheat broiler to low. Slice each hoagie roll in half. Drizzle each half with olive oil and rub 1 clove of garlic over each half. Toast under broiler for 3–5 minutes, or until slightly toasted. Remove bread, but keep broiler heated.

In a small skillet, cook sausage until crumbled and no longer pink (about 5 minutes). Add mushrooms. Cook an additional 3–4 minutes or until mushrooms begin to soften.

Arrange turkey, ham, and salami over bottom half of each roll (about 2 slices of each meat). Top deli meat with two slices of provolone cheese. Divide cooked mushrooms and sausage over cheese. Top cheese with marinara sauce (about 2 tablespoons per roll).

Broil sandwiches on high 2–4 minutes, or until cheese has melted and meat is warm. Arrange hoagie tops on sandwiches.

# beer cheese and brat pretzel sandwich

*Everyone wants to be a little German during Oktoberfest! This a fun spin on traditional German cuisine!*

Prep time: 5 minutes | Cook time: 21 minutes | Makes: 4 sandwiches

BRATS

1 package brats, such as Johnsonville
1 tablespoon olive oil

BEER CHEESE

2 tablespoons of butter
2 tablespoons of flour
¼ cup beer
1 cup shredded cheddar
½ teaspoon mustard

1 (14-oz.) can sauerkraut, drained

4 pretzel buns

Fill a large, deep skillet with ½ inch of water. Prick brats with a fork a few times to allow steam to escape while cooking. Simmer brats covered for 20 minutes. Drain any liquid. Add oil to hot pan and place brats to brown for 1 minute. Remove brats and let cool slightly. Slice each brat lengthwise.

To make the beer cheese, melt butter in a small saucepan. Add flour and whisk until smooth. Stir in beer, cheese, and mustard. Keep stirring over low heat until cheese is melted and smooth.

To assemble, place sliced brats on the bottom of each pretzel bun. Divide sauerkraut among each sandwich. Drizzle beer cheese over top.

# poblano, brie, and cherry grilled cheese

*Smoky poblano peppers are the perfect counterpart for sweet cherry preserves. The creamy brie brings them all together!*

Prep time: 4 minutes | Cook time: 12 minutes | Makes: 2 sandwiches

- ½ teaspoon olive oil
- 1 whole poblano pepper, sliced
- 1 clove garlic minced
- ⅛ teaspoon salt
- 2 teaspoons butter
- 4 slices hearty white bread
- 4 slices brie cheese (rinds removed)
- 2 generous tablespoons cherry preserves
- 4-6 slices poblano per sandwich

Heat olive oil in a skillet over medium heat. Add poblano peppers. Cook peppers for 3 minutes. Add garlic and salt. Cook an additional minute. Remove from heat.

Spread a ½ teaspoon butter on one side of each piece of bread. Place two slices of bread buttered side down on a hot grill pan. Top with two slices of brie and a tablespoon of preserves on each sandwich, followed by pepper slices. Cover with remaining bread, buttered side up.

Cook sandwiches for 4–6 minutes per side or until toasted.

# crab cake sandwich with artichokes and crème fraîche

*One of my favorite appetizers to order is crab cakes. The problem is you never get enough! I created my own version to enjoy any time the craving strikes.*

Prep time: 1 hour | Cook time: 16 minutes | Makes: 4 sandwiches

8 oz. lump crab meat
¼ cup mayonnaise
1 egg, lightly beaten
1 teaspoon lemon juice
¼ teaspoon salt
1 tablespoon parsley
¾ cup Panko Japanese bread crumbs
1 tablespoon butter
4 small sandwich rolls
4 tablespoons chopped marinated artichoke hearts
¼ cup crème fraîche
2 teaspoons fresh tarragon

In a bowl, combine crab meat and mayonnaise. Stir in egg, lemon juice, and salt. Add parsley and Panko and stir until combined. Do not overmix. Refrigerate mixture for 1 hour.

In a large skillet, melt 1 tablespoon butter over medium heat. Shape crab mixture into 4 patties and cook for 5–8 minutes per side, or until golden brown.

Place one crab cake on the bottom of each sandwich roll. Top with 1 tablespoon chopped artichokes and one tablespoon of crème fraîche. Sprinkle ½ teaspoon of fresh tarragon over each crab cake. Top with roll top.

# spicy apricot pork sandwich with honey lime slaw

*This smoky sweet pork and zest slaw will be requested at every BBQ!*

Prep time: 10 minutes | Cook time: 3 hours | Makes: 8 sandwiches

APRICOT PORK

3 lb. pork tenderloin
2 teaspoons olive oil
2 cloves garlic minced
1 cup ketchup
¾ cup apricot preserves
½ cup brown sugar
¼ cup cider vinegar
¼ cup cayenne pepper sauce
1 teaspoon cumin
½ teaspoon salt
1 tablespoon Worcestershire sauce

SLAW

2 cups shredded red cabbage
1 tablespoon chopped cilantro
1 tablespoon honey
1 large lime, squeezed
¼ teaspoon salt

8 onion rolls

Place pork tenderloin in a slow cooker. In a bowl, combine olive oil, garlic, ketchup, preserves, and next 6 ingredients. Stir and pour over pork. Cover and cook pork on high for 3 hours. Shred fully cooked pork.

For the slaw, place cabbage in a bowl. Add cilantro, honey, lime, and salt. Toss to coat.

Divide pork among each roll and top with slaw.

# kale and brussels sprouts stuffed pita sandwich

*Salty pancetta, crunchy brussels sprouts, and creamy blue cheese make this light pita sandwich irresistible!*

Prep time: 10 minutes | Makes: 4 pita halves

SALAD

8 oz. brussels sprouts, thinly sliced
2 oz. pancetta, chopped
3 cups tightly packed curly leaf kale
2 tablespoons blue cheese, crumbled

VINAIGRETTE

2 tablespoons chopped shallot
1 teaspoon coarse mustard
2 tablespoons red wine vinegar
¼ cup olive oil
½ teaspoon salt

2 whole pita bread rounds, cut in half

In a bowl, toss together the brussels sprouts, pancetta, kale, and blue cheese.

Prepare the dressing by whisking together shallots, mustard, vinegar, olive oil, and salt. Pour dressing over salad. Toss to coat.

Stuff salad inside each pita. Serve.

# the meat loaf sandwich

*In my opinion, the best thing about meat loaf is using leftovers for sandwiches!*

**Prep time: 10 minutes | Cook time: 35 minutes | Makes: 4 sandwiches**

## MEAT LOAF PATTIES

1 lb. ground beef
1 egg
¼ teaspoon garlic salt
1 tablespoon Worcestershire sauce
2 tablespoons chopped parsley
½ cup Italian bread crumbs

## SAUCE

4 tablespoons ketchup
1 tablespoon mustard
1 clove garlic, chopped
1 tablespoon brown sugar

8 slices whole grain bread
4 teaspoons stone ground mustard
4 pieces of green lettuce

Preheat oven to 350 degrees.

In a bowl, stir together beef, egg, salt, Worcestershire sauce, parsley, and bread crumbs. Mix until combined (do not overmix!). Shape beef into 4 patties. Place patties on a baking a dish that has been sprayed with nonstick spray. Bake patties for 35 minutes, or until done.

In a small bowl, stir together ketchup, mustard, garlic, and brown sugar.

Spread ½ teaspoon of stone ground mustard over each slice of bread. Place a piece of lettuce over 4 slices of bread. Rest patty over lettuce and drizzle ketchup mixture over each patty. Top with remaining slice of bread.

# fried green tomato BLT

*The first time I had a fried green tomato was during a trip to South Carolina. I can't eat a BLT without one! This version turns your ordinary BLT on its head! This sandwich features two kinds tomatoes: fried green and sun dried. It also has crisp spinach as a stand-in for plain old lettuce!*

**Prep time: 5 minutes | Cook time: 20 minutes | Makes: 4 sandwiches**

### TOMATO

- 2 tablespoons corn oil
- ¼ cup flour
- ¾ cup cornmeal
- 2 teaspoons Old Bay seasoning
- 1 egg, lightly beaten
- 2 tablespoons buttermilk
- 2 green tomatoes, sliced into 4 slices

### MAYONNAISE

- ½ cup mayonnaise
- ¼ cup chopped oil-packed sun dried tomatoes

- 8 slices sourdough bread
- 1 cup spinach
- 8 strips of cooked bacon

Heat oil in a large skillet over medium heat.

Combine flour, cornmeal, and seasoning in a bowl. Combine egg and buttermilk in a separate bowl. Dredge tomato slices in egg mixture and then dip in cornmeal mixture. Shake off excess cornmeal mixture and place tomatoes in hot oil. Fry tomatoes for 5 minutes per side, or until golden and crispy. Work in batches as necessary. Place tomatoes on a paper towel lined baking sheet to drain.

Combine mayonnaise and chopped tomatoes in a small bowl.

Spread mayonnaise on each slice of bread. Top 4 slices of bread with ¼ cup spinach. Cover spinach with two tomato slices, two strips of bacon, and remaining slices of bread.

# philly cheesesteak patty melt

*Patty melts are diner food at its best! Thin patties are key to these sandwiches!*

**Prep time: 5 minutes | Cook time: 30 minutes | Makes: 4 sandwiches**

- 1 lb. lean ground beef
- 2 teaspoons olive oil, divided
- 1 large green pepper, sliced
- 1 small red onion, cut into rings
- ¼ teaspoon salt
- ½ teaspoon oregano
- 4 tablespoons sliced provolone
- 4 teaspoons mayonnaise
- 8 slices sourdough bread

Shape ground beef into 4 thin patties.

Heat 1 teaspoon of olive oil in a skillet over medium-high heat. Add patties and cook 6–8 minutes per side. Remove patties and keep warm.

Wipe the same skillet with a paper towel and return to heat. Add remaining teaspoon of olive oil and heat over medium heat. Add pepper and onions to skillet and season with salt and oregano. Cook veggies for 8–10 minutes or until soft. Remove veggie mixture.

Wipe skillet one last time. Top 4 slices of bread with provolone cheese. Place one beef patty over cheese slices and divide pepper mixture over patties. Place remaining bread slices over pepper mixture.

Spread ½ teaspoon of mayo over bread. Place sandwich mayonnaise-side down onto hot skillet. Spread remaining mayonnaise on top side of bread. Cook sandwiches for about 3 minutes, or until golden. Flip and cook second side an additional 3 minutes.

# cuban stromboli

Stromboli *is a fun word to say, but it's even more fun to eat! This is a quick and easy take on a Cuban sandwich.*

Prep time: 10 minutes | Cook time: 25 minutes | Makes: 6

1 teaspoon olive oil
½ lb. ground pork sausage
1 (13.8-oz) tube refrigerated pizza dough (unbaked)
¾ cup shredded swiss cheese
5 slices black forest ham
8 sandwich-style dill pickles
2 tablespoons Dijon mustard
1 tablespoon butter
½ teaspoon garlic salt

Preheat oven to 375 degrees.

Heat oil in skillet. Add ground pork. Cook until no longer pink, crumbling as it cooks. Drain pork on a paper towel and let cool completely.

Place dough on a floured surface and roll out to 14 × 12-inch rectangle. Sprinkle with cheese, a layer of ham, pickles, a drizzle of Dijon mustard, and pork. Roll up stromboli starting with the long end and place roll seam side down on an ungreased baking sheet. Pinch ends together.

Brush roll with melted butter and sprinkle with garlic salt.

Bake for 20–25 minutes, or until golden brown. Let stand for 3–5 minutes before slicing.

# vegetarian muffaletta subs

*I've taken the best part of a Muffaletta sandwich and made a vegetarian version!*

**Prep time: 10 minutes | Cook time: 5 minutes | Makes: 6 sandwiches**

1 whole head cauliflower
pinch of salt and pepper
½ cup chopped black olives
½ cup chopped green olives
½ cup diced jarred red bell pepper
¼ cup chopped pepperoncini peppers
1 tablespoon olive oil
6 sub rolls
4 teaspoons mayonnaise
8 slices provolone cheese

Preheat grill (or grill pan) and spray with a nonstick spray. Slice cauliflower head into 1-inch thick slices. Grill cauliflower slices for 3–4 minutes per side. Remove and let cool. Coarsely chop cauliflower into bite-size pieces.

In a bowl, combine olives, red bell pepper, pepperoncini, cauliflower, and olive oil. Toss to coat.

Slice each sub roll (taking care not to slice all the way through). Spread mayonnaise on the inside of each roll. Divide olive salad evenly among each roll. Place one and half slices of provolone cheese on each sub roll.

Preheat broiler and broil subs on low for 3–5 minutes or until cheese has melted.

# grilled chicago dog sandwich

*Summertime wouldn't be complete without a good ol' Chicago dog! This grilled version just might take its place!*

Prep time: 5 minutes | Cook time: 6 minutes | Makes: 2 sandwiches

2 teaspoons butter
4 slices poppy seed or multigrain bread
2 all-beef hot dogs
4 slices white American cheese

TOPPINGS

2 onion slices
1 roma tomato, sliced (6 slices)
4 sandwich size dill pickles
1 teaspoon yellow mustard
½ teaspoon celery salt

Heat a grill pan over medium heat. Cook hot dogs according to package directions. Let cool until easy to handle. Spread butter on one side of each piece of bread. Place two bread slices butter-side down on grill pan.

Slice hot dogs down the center lengthwise. Place one slice of cheese on each slice of bread, followed by two hot dog halves, onions, tomato slices, pickles, mustard, and celery salt. Place remaining cheese slices on top, followed by second slice of bread (buttered side up).

Toast sandwich for 2–3 minutes per side, or until golden.

# turkey monte cristo

*A little sweet, a little savory, and wholly delicious!*

Prep time: 5 minutes | Cook time: 15 minutes | Makes: 2 sandwiches

SAUCE

6 oz. fresh raspberries
2 tablespoons sugar
2 tablespoons water
splash of lemon juice

SANDWICH

2 eggs, lightly beaten
¼ cup milk
4 slices sweet, Hawaiian style bread
4 slices deli turkey
½ cup shredded Gruyère cheese
1 tablespoon butter

powdered sugar

Prepare the sauce by combining the raspberries, sugar, water, and lemon juice in a small saucepan. Bring to a boil, reduce heat, and simmer for 6–8 minutes, or until berries have broken down and sauce has thickened.

Meanwhile, prepare the sandwich. Heat a grill pan over medium heat. Melt butter on hot pan.

In a bowl, whisk together the eggs and the milk. Sandwich two slices of turkey and ¼ cup Gruyère cheese between two slice of bread. Dip sandwich in egg mixture and place on hot grill pan.

Brown sandwich for 4–6 minutes per side, or until egg is cooked and bread is golden.

Serve with raspberry sauce and sprinkle with sugar if desired.

# spicy peppered portobello burgers

*Who needs beef? Thick portobello burgers make excellent beef stand-ins. The spicy pepper mixture adds a little southwestern flair to these vegetarian burgers!*

Prep time: 3 minutes | Cook time: 10 minutes | Makes: 2 sandwiches

JALAPEÑO MAYONNAISE

¼ cup mayonnaise
1 tablespoon chopped fresh jalapeño
1 clove garlic, minced
¼ teaspoon salt
pinch of pepper

PEPPERS

1 teaspoon olive oil
2 tablespoons chopped onion
1 (4-oz.) can diced green chiles, drained
⅛ teaspoon cumin

½ teaspoon olive oil
¼ teaspoon salt
2 large portobello mushroom caps
2 slices pepper jack cheese
2 hamburger buns
lettuce, tomato, and avocado

In a bowl, combine mayonnaise, jalapeño, garlic, salt, and pepper.

Preheat broiler.

First prepare your peppers by heating 1 teaspoon of olive oil in a small skillet. Add chopped onion, green chiles, and cumin to onion mixture. Cook over medium heat for 2–3 minutes, or until onions are translucent. Remove from heat.

For the mushrooms, preheat a grill pan over medium heat. Rub olive oil and salt over both mushrooms. Grill mushrooms 3–4 minutes per side, or until tender. Place mushrooms on a broiler-safe baking sheet. Top each mushroom with one slice of cheese. Place mushrooms under broiler until cheese is melted (about 1 minute).

Generously slather jalapeño mayonnaise over inside of each bun. Place portobello on bottoms of the hamburger buns. Top each with lettuce, tomato, avocado, and chile mixture.

# spinach and artichoke grilled cheese

*Your favorite appetizer is now a meal!*

Prep time: 5 minutes | Cook time: 6 minutes | Makes: 4 sandwiches

- 6 oz. marinated artichoke hearts, drained
- 5 oz. frozen spinach, thawed and drained
- ½ cup mayonnaise
- 1 clove garlic
- ½ teaspoon salt
- ½ teaspoon oregano
- ¾ cup shredded Monterey Jack cheese
- 4 teaspoons butter
- 8 slices Italian bread

In a bowl, combine artichokes, spinach, mayonnaise, garlic, salt, oregano, and Monterey Jack cheese.

Heat a grill pan over medium heat. Place ½ teaspoon of butter on one side of each slice of bread. Place 4 sandwiches buttered side down on hot grill pan. Divide artichoke mixture over each bread half and top with second slice of bread buttered side up.

Toast each sandwich 3–4 minutes per side, or until golden. Remove and serve.

# buffalo shrimp po boy

*New York meets Louisiana in this simple take on a classic sandwich.*

Prep time: 5 minutes | Cook time: 4 minutes | Makes: 4 sandwiches

SHRIMP

1 teaspoon olive oil
1 lb. jumbo shrimp
¼ teaspoon seasoning salt
1 tablespoon butter
¼ cup buffalo wing sauce

SLAW

1 cup shredded lettuce
¼ teaspoon salt
1 celery stalk, finely chopped
2 tablespoons chopped green onions
4 oz. crumbled blue cheese
2 tablespoons white vinegar

4 hoagie buns

TOPPINGS

2 roma tomatoes, sliced
8 sandwich-style dill pickle slices
hot sauce (optional)

Heat olive oil in a skillet over medium low heat. Add peeled shrimp seasoned with seasoning salt. Cook 3–4 minute, or until shrimp have turned pink. Do not overcook.

In a bowl, melt butter and stir in buffalo wing sauce. Add cooked shrimp. Set aside.

In a small bowl, combine lettuce, salt, celery, green onions, blue cheese, and vinegar. Stir to coat.

To assemble, split each hoagie bun. Place shrimp on hoagies and top with tomato slices, 2 pickle slices, and about ¼ cup of slaw.

# roast beef croissant with pickled shallots

*Hearty roast beef and piquant white cheddar combine beautifully with tangy pickled shallots!*

Prep time: 5 minutes | Makes: 4 croissants

- 1 extra large shallot, thinly sliced
- ½ cup cider vinegar
- ¼ cup sugar
- 1 teaspoon salt
- ¼ cup mayonnaise
- ¾ lb. thinly sliced deli roast beef
- 4 slices white cheddar
- 1 cup loosely packed baby kale
- 2 tablespoons stone ground mustard
- 4 large croissants, cut in half

To prepare the sliced shallots, place them in bowl. Add vinegar, sugar, and salt. Stir. Set aside while you assemble the sandwich.

Place 1 tablespoon of mayonnaise on the bottom of each croissant. Layer 2–3 slices of roast beef over mayo, followed by cheddar cheese. Place ¼ cup of kale over cheese. Divide pickled shallots among each sandwich. Spread ½ tablespoon of mustard on the tops of each croissant and place over shallots. Serve.

# vegetarian bánh mì

*This traditional Vietnamese sandwich is often made with chicken or pork. You won't miss either with this hearty vegetarian version.*

**Prep time: 30 minutes–24 hours | Cook time: 8 minutes | Makes: 2–4 sandwiches**

PICKLED VEGETABLES

½ cup shredded carrot
½ cup Daikon radish, shredded
½ cup rice vinegar
¼ cup water
¼ cup sugar
pinch of salt

MUSHROOMS

2 teaspoons vegetable oil
8 oz. sliced portobello mushroom slices
1 teaspoon jarred ginger
2 tablespoons soy sauce

TOPPINGS

3 tablespoons mayonnaise
1 clove garlic, minced
1 teaspoon Sriracha
10–12 thin slices of cucumber
1 jalapeño, sliced
2 tablespoons chopped cilantro

2 French baguettes (6 oz. each) or 1 large (12-oz.) baguette

In a bowl, combine carrots, shredded radish, vinegar, water, sugar, and salt, stirring to coat. Cover with plastic wrap and refrigerate for at least one hour or overnight. The longer they sit, the better.

Heat 2 teaspoons of vegetable oil in a large skillet over medium heat. Add portobello mushrooms, ginger, and soy sauce; stir. Continue to cook mushrooms for 5–8 minutes, or until soft. Remove from heat and set aside.

Meanwhile, combine mayonnaise, garlic, and Sriracha in a small bowl.

To assemble, split baguette lengthwise, but do not cut all the way through. Place mushrooms inside baguette. Place cucumber slices alongside mushroom. Divide carrot mixture over baguette. Drizzle mayonnaise mixture over the sandwich and place jalapeño slices over mayonnaise. Sprinkle with cilantro. Cut baguette in half before serving.

# dagwood for a crowd

*Get ready to eat! This sandwich is not for the faint of heart. It is the perfect sandwich to feed a crowd!*

Prep time: 15 minutes | Serves: 6–8

- 1 round light rye bread loaf (16 oz.)
- 4 tablespoons mayonnaise
- ½ cup loosely packed spinach
- 4 slices cheddar cheese
- 6 slices deli ham
- 1 small cucumber, cut into 12 slices (divided)
- 6 slices cooked bacon, divided
- 6 slices beef steak tomatoes
- 4 slices provolone cheese
- 6 slices hard salami
- 4 tablespoons stone ground mustard
- 1 cup spring mix lettuce
- 4 slices pepper jack cheese
- 6 slices sandwich pepperoni
- 1 avocado, sliced
- 4 slices Muenster cheese
- 6 slices deli turkey
- olives and toothpicks for garnish

Cut round loaf horizontally into 3 sections.

Spread bottom round with 2 tablespoons of mayonnaise. Cover mayo with spinach. Arrange 4 slices of cheddar cheese over spinach, followed by deli ham. Arrange 6 slices of cucumber over cheese, followed by 3 slices of bacon and 3 slices of tomato. Place 4 slices of provolone cheese over tomatoes, followed by 6 slices of hard salami.

Place middle section of bread over salami. Spread mustard over the top of bread. Arrange lettuce over mustard, followed by pepper jack, pepperoni, 6 slices of cucumber, and remaining bacon. Place avocado slices over bacon. Arrange Muenster cheese over bacon, followed by deli turkey.

Spread remaining mayonnaise on the underside of the top of the loaf and place on the sandwich.

Cover in plastic wrap until ready to serve. Place olive garnish in the center of the sandwich just before serving.

# chicken alfredo sandwich

*Who needs pasta? This sandwich has everything you love about a good chicken Alfredo dish!*

Prep time: 5 minutes | Cook time: 21 minutes | Makes: 5–6 sandwiches

1 teaspoon olive oil
½ lb. chicken tenders
salt and pepper
2 cloves garlic, minced
3 tablespoons butter
3 tablespoons flour
1½ cups milk
2 oz. cream cheese
½ teaspoon salt
¼ cup Italian blend shredded cheese
¼ cup Parmesan cheese
Italian bread sliced into 10–12 pieces

Heat oil in a skillet over medium heat. Sprinkle chicken tenders with salt and pepper and place chicken in skillet. Cook chicken for 4 minutes per side. Remove and let chicken cool.

Meanwhile, melt butter in a small saucepan. Whisk in flour and let cook for 1 minute. Whisk in milk, taking care to rid sauce of any lumps. Add cream cheese and continue to whisk until cream cheese is fully incorporated. Season cheese sauce with salt and add shredded cheese. Whisk until smooth and creamy.

Preheat oven to 350 degrees. Toast bread for 6–8 minutes, turning once. Remove bread slices from oven and set the oven to broil.

Halve each chicken tender and place two tenders on half of the bread slices. Spoon cheese sauce over chicken. Broil for 3 minutes, or until cheese is golden and bubbly. Top cheese and chicken with remaining bread slices. Serve.

# honey balsamic salmon with edamame spread

*Edamame makes such a creamy spread. It's the perfect counterpart to the seasoned salmon!*

Prep time: 15 minutes | Cook time: 12 minutes | Makes: 4 sandwiches

SPREAD

12 oz. shelled edamame
2 cloves of garlic
¾ teaspoons salt
3 tablespoons olive oil
2 tablespoons lemon juice
¼ cup parsley
¼ cup sour cream
¼ cup water

SALMON

1 lb. salmon
½ teaspoon salt, pepper
3 tablespoons mayonnaise
1 oz. crumbled goat cheese
2 tablespoons honey
1 tablespoon balsamic vinegar

1 loaf ciabatta, halved horizontally
4 leaves, red leaf lettuce leaves

Cook edamame according to package directions. Let cool.

In a food processor, combine edamame, garlic, salt, olive oil, lemon juice, parsley, and sour cream. Add water one tablespoon at a time, checking your consistency after each addition. Process until completely smooth.

Preheat oven to 450. Arrange salmon on a baking sheet sprinkle with salt and pepper. Bake salmon for 12 minutes.

In a small bowl, combine mayonnaise and goat cheese. Set aside.

In a separate small bowl, microwave honey until thin. Add balsamic vinegar and stir. Set aside.

To assemble sandwich, spread edamame spread over the bottom of the ciabatta bread. Top with red leaf lettuce. Place salmon over lettuce and drizzle with honey mixture. Top second ciabatta half with mayo and goat cheese. Place over salmon.

Cut loaf into 4 sandwiches. Serve.

# beef stroganoff rolls

*Beef stroganoff is pure comfort food! These little bundles take comfort to a portable level!*

Prep time: 20 minutes | Cook time: 10 minutes | Makes: 8 rolls

BEEF

- 2 teaspoons olive oil
- 1 small shallot, chopped
- 1 clove garlic, minced
- 1 lb. sirloin steak cut into bite-sized chunks
- 1 cup finely chopped mushrooms
- 1 tablespoon Worcestershire sauce
- ¼ teaspoon salt
- ⅛ teaspoon pepper

ROLLS

- 4 oz cream cheese, softened
- 1 tablespoon Dijon mustard
- 1 teaspoon fresh dill, chopped
- 2 (16.3-oz.) jumbo biscuits
- 2 tablespoons melted butter
- 1 teaspoon garlic powder

Heat olive oil in a skillet over medium heat. Add shallots and cook for 2 minutes or until shallots begin to soften. Add garlic and cook for 1 minute. Add beef to skillet. Cook for 2–3 minutes, or until no longer pink. Stir in mushrooms, Worcestershire sauce, salt, and pepper. Stir and cook until slightly thick. Remove from heat and let mixture cool.

In a bowl, combine cream cheese, mustard, and dill.

Preheat oven to 425 degrees. Unroll biscuits from tube. Spread each biscuit into flat rounds. Place a tablespoon of cheese mixture onto each biscuit. Place a generous spoonful of beef over cheese. Pull up edges of biscuits and pinch together. Carefully roll biscuit into a ball in your hands and place on a baking sheet, gathered side down. Brush each roll with melted butter and sprinkle with garlic powder.

Bake rolls for 8–10 minutes, or until golden brown.

# sweet sammies

***"Too few people understand a really good sandwich."***
***—James Beard***

# peanut butter–filled chocolate sandwich cookies

*Chocolate and peanut butter are happy companions in these easy sandwich cookies!*

Prep time: 25 minutes | Cook time: 8 minutes | Makes: 6 sandwiches

4 oz. semisweet chocolate
1 tablespoon butter
2 tablespoons flour
⅛ teaspoon baking powder
⅛ teaspoon salt
1 egg
⅓ cup sugar
½ teaspoon vanilla

FROSTING

3 tablespoons softened butter
⅓ cup creamy peanut butter
¾ cup powdered sugar
1 teaspoon vanilla
1 ½ tablespoons cream
2 tablespoons mini chocolate chips

In a small saucepan, combine chocolate and butter. Cook over low heat until both have melted. Stir until smooth and set aside.

In a small bowl, combine flour, baking powder, and salt. Set aside.

In a mixing bowl, beat together the eggs, sugar, and vanilla until mixture begins to thicken. Stir in cooled chocolate mixture, followed by flour mixture. Beat until combined. Let batter stand for 10 minutes in order to thicken up.

Preheat oven to 375 degrees. Drop dough by tablespoon onto a lined baking sheet, keeping each cookie about 2 inches apart. Bake for 8 minutes, or until edges are set and cookies are slightly cracked. Let cool for 1 minute before removing to a cooling rack.

Prepare the frosting. In a mixer bowl, combine butter and peanut butter, beating until smooth. Slowly mix in powdered sugar one cup at a time, mixing well after each addition. Add in vanilla and cream and beat until frosting is spreadable consistency, adding more cream if necessary. Stir in mini chocolate chips.

To assemble, pipe or spread a generous spoonful of frosting over the bottoms of 6 cookies. Top each with remaining cookies.

# tiramisu pastry sandwiches

*These puff pastry sandwiches are an easy, quick take on one of my favorite desserts: tiramisu!*

Prep time: 10 minutes | Cook time: 15 minutes | Makes: 12 sandwiches

- 1 (17.3-oz.) box puffed pastry sheets
- 8 oz. mascarpone cheese, softened
- 1 (8-oz.) block cream cheese, softened
- ⅓ cup brown sugar
- ¼ cup granulated sugar
- 4 tablespoons Kahlua liqueur
- 2 tablespoons coffee
- ½ semisweet chocolate chips
- 1 teaspoon shortening
- powdered sugar and cocoa powder for dusting

Preheat oven to 400 degrees. Cut each sheet of pastry dough into six equal pieces and place on a baking sheet. Bake for 15 minutes, or until golden. Remove from oven and cool completely.

Prepare the filling by place mascarpone and cream cheese in the bowl of mixer. Beat until cheeses are creamy and smooth. Add both sugars to cheese. Continue to mix until combined. Stir in liqueur and coffee.

When pastry has cooled, cut each pastry in half and brush coffee mixture on inside of each half. Spread 2 tablespoons of filling on bottom half.

In a microwave-safe bowl, melt chocolate and shortening together in 30-second intervals until smooth. Place chocolate in a plastic bag. Snip one corner of the bag and drizzle chocolate over filling. Replace top. Dust pastries with powdered sugar and cocoa powder. Serve.

# key lime pie ice cream sandwiches

*Graham crackers are just the thing to surround the pucker-liscious key lime ice cream!*

Prep time: 1 hour–24 hours | Makes: 9 Ice Cream Sandwiches

- 1 (4-oz.) container egg product (such as Egg Beaters)
- 1 cup granulated sugar
- 2 cups heavy cream
- 1 cup half and half
- ½ teaspoon vanilla
- ⅓ cup key lime juice
- 1 tablespoon key lime zest
- 9 graham crackers, broken into squares (18 total)

In a blender, combine egg product and sugar. Add heavy cream, half and half, vanilla, key lime juice, and zest. Blend until completely mixed. Refrigerate for at least an hour or up to 24 hours.

Pour ice cream into the bowl of an ice cream maker and prepare according to manufacturer's directions.

Line an 8 × 8-inch pan with plastic wrap with at least 2 inches hanging over the side. Pour ice cream onto plastic wrap and freeze until completely set (at least one hour or up to 24 hours).

When ice cream is ready, arrange 9 graham crackers over the top of the ice cream. Place a plate or a baking sheet over the top of the ice cream. Carefully invert ice cream onto the plate Remove plastic wrap and arrange remaining graham crackers over the ice cream. Refreeze if necessary.

After ice cream has set, carefully cut ice cream into 9 equal squares. Wrap each sandwich with plastic. Place ice cream sandwiches back in the freezer to set or serve immediately.

# pistachio cherry cupcake sandwiches

*Having the filling sandwiched between two cupcake halves ensures that frosting and cake is in every single bite!*

Prep time: 20 minutes | Cook time: 18 minutes | Makes: 16 cupcakes

- 1 stick of butter, softened
- 1 cup sugar
- ½ cup milk
- 1 teaspoon vanilla
- 1½ cups cake flour
- 1 tablespoon baking powder
- 3 egg whites
- ½ cup pistachios
- ¼ cup powdered sugar
- ¼ cup butter, softened
- ¼ cup shortening
- 2 cups powdered sugar
- pinch of salt
- ¼ maraschino cherry juice
- 1 tablespoon heavy cream
- ¼ cup chopped maraschino cherries

Preheat oven to 350 degrees. Line 2 cupcake tins with paper liners and set aside.

In a stand mixer, beat butter until creamy. Add in sugar and beat until fluffy.

Combine milk and vanilla in a measuring cup. Set aside.

Stir together flour and baking powder. Carefully add ¼ of the flour mixture to butter mixture alternately with a ¼ of the milk mixture, beginning and ending with the flour.

In a separate bowl, beat egg white at medium speed until stiff peaks form. Slowly and carefully fold egg whites into cupcake batter. Toss pistachios with powdered sugar, and fold nuts into cupcake batter.

Fill each cupcake liner ⅔ full. Bake for 18 minutes, or until a toothpick inserted comes out clean. Let cupcakes cool completely.

For the filling, beat butter and shortening together until creamy. Add powdered sugar 1 cup at a time. Add a pinch of salt and cherry juice. Continue to beat until smooth. Beat in heavy cream and cherries.

Split cupcakes in half. Pipe or spoon filling onto bottom half of each cupcake. Place cupcake top over filling. Serve.

# mocha donut sandwich

*If you haven't had a profiterole, know that it's an airy little pastry that is often filled with a scoop of ice cream and drizzled with sauce. This is my lazy-man's version!*

Prep time: 6 minutes | Cook time: 2 minutes | Makes: 4 Sandwiches

3 oz. unsweetened chocolate
⅓ cup heavy cream
½ cup sugar
2 tablespoons butter
1 teaspoon vanilla
2 tablespoons Irish cream
4 glazed donuts split in half horizontally
4 scoops coffee ice cream

Prepare the chocolate sauce by stirring together chocolate and heavy cream in a microwave-safe bowl. Heat for 1½ minutes, or until chocolate has melted. Stir until smooth. Add sugar and return chocolate to microwave. Heat an additional 3 minutes, stirring after 1 ½ minutes. Heat until sugar has dissolved. Stir in butter, vanilla, and Irish cream. Stir until well blended.

Spray a grill pan with nonstick spray and heat over medium-low heat. Add sliced donuts and heat for 1 minute per side, or until soft.

Place 4 donut bottoms on 4 plates. Place one scoop of ice cream onto each donut half. Top with donut top and drizzle with chocolate sauce.

# grilled biscoff and banana fluffernutter sandwich

*Move over, peanut butter—Biscoff spread makes a sophisticated version of a childhood favorite!*

Prep time: 2 minutes | Cook time: 6 minutes | Makes: 4 sandwiches

- 8 (1-inch) slices ciabatta bread
- 4 teaspoons butter
- 4 tablespoons Biscoff spread (cookie butter spread)
- 1 whole banana, sliced
- 4 tablespoons marshmallow fluff

Heat a grill pan over medium heat. Butter one side of each piece of bread with a ½ teaspoon of butter. Place 4 bread slices, buttered side down, onto hot pan. Place 1 tablespoon of Biscoff spread onto each piece of bread. Place 2–3 slices of banana over Biscoff, followed by 1 tablespoon of marshmallow fluff. Place remaining bread slices over marshmallow fluff, buttered side up.

Toast sandwiches for 2–3 minutes, or until toasted. Carefully flip sandwiches and toast second side.

# pizzelles with peach and cinnamon mascarpone sandwiches

*Delicate pizzelle cookies, light mascarpone filling, and sweet peaches melt in your mouth with each luscious bite!*

Prep time: 15 minutes | Cook time: 8 minutes | Makes: 12–13 sandwiches

PEACHES

4 large peaches, sliced
2 tablespoons butter, melted
½ teaspoon honey

FILLING

8 oz. mascarpone cheese, softened
8 oz. cream cheese, softened
1½ cups powdered sugar
½ teaspoon vanilla
½ teaspoon cinnamon
1 tablespoon heavy cream

1 (7-oz.) package pizzelle cookies (thin waffle cone cookies found in the bakery section of your grocery store)

Toss together peaches, butter, and honey. Heat a grill pan over medium heat. Add peaches to pan and grill for 5–8 minutes, or until peaches are warm and tender. Remove peaches from heat and set aside.

For the filling, in the bowl of a mixer, combine mascarpone and cream cheese. Beat together cheeses until creamy and smooth. Carefully stir in powdered sugar a half a cup at a time. Mix in vanilla, cinnamon, and heavy cream until well blended.

To assemble sandwiches, top one waffle cookie with two tablespoons of filling and two peach slices. Top with another cookie. Serve immediately.

# caramel and marshmallow wafer sandwiches

*Homemade marshmallows are so easy to make and are like nothing you've ever tasted! The wafers and simple caramel sauce make for a unique and indulgent treat!*

Prep time: 4½ hours | Makes: 18 sandwiches

MARSHMALLOWS

- 3 (¼-oz.) package unflavored gelatin
- 1 cup ice water, divided
- 1½ cups granulated sugar
- 1 cup corn syrup
- ⅛ teaspoon salt
- 2 teaspoons vanilla
- ¼ cup powdered sugar
- ¼ cup cornstarch

CARAMEL SAUCE

- ½ cup brown sugar
- ¼ cup heavy cream
- 2 tablespoons butter
- 1 teaspoon vanilla
- ½ teaspoon sea salt

36 chocolate wafer cookies

Place gelatin and ½ cup ice water in a stand mixer that has been fitted with a whisk attachment.

Meanwhile, combine sugar, corn syrup, salt, and remaining ½ cup ice water in a small saucepan over medium heat. Cook and stir the mixture over medium heat until sugar dissolves. Increase temperature and cook without stirring until a candy thermometer clipped to the side of the pan registers 240 degrees. Remove from heat.

Begin whisking your gelatin mixture on low speed. Slowly and carefully stream in syrup mixture. When all the syrup has been added, increase mixer speed to high and whip until mixture is light and fluffy and the bowl temperature has reduced to lukewarm. This should take anywhere from 5–10 minutes. When marshmallow mixture has thickened and becomes glossy, add vanilla. Whip just until incorporated.

Spray a 9 × 13-inch pan with nonstick spray. Combine powdered sugar and cornstarch in a small bowl. Pour half of the sugar mixture on your pan and rotate pan so that the sugar covers the bottom and the sides. Spray a spatula with nonstick spray and spread your marshmallow onto your pan. Pour remaining sugar mixture over marshmallow and spread out using your fingers.

Cover and let stand at least 4 hours.

Meanwhile, cook brown sugar, heavy cream, and butter on medium for 5–7 minutes, or until thick and amber in color. Remove and add vanilla and salt to the caramel mixture.

Cut marshmallows with a 3-inch cookie cutter that has been dipped in powdered sugar. Place one marshmallow on each of the 18 chocolate wafers. Place a half teaspoon of caramel on each marshmallow and top with remaining wafers. Serve immediately.

*If you do not own a candy thermometer, after cooking the sugar mixture for about 8 minutes, drop a spoonful of sugar mixture into a bowl of cold water. If sugar forms a ball, the mixture is ready.

# roasted strawberry hazelnut sandwich

*Roasted berries become an intensely sweet and flavorful contrast to the rich and smooth hazelnut spread.*

Prep time: 15 minutes | Cook time: 6 minutes | Makes: 6 sandwiches

1 lb. strawberries, quartered
2 tablespoons brown sugar
1 teaspoon vanilla
1 (16-oz.) loaf Challah bread (sliced about 1 inch thick)
6 teaspoons butter
6 teaspoons turbinado sugar
12 tablespoons hazelnut spread

Preheat oven to 400 degrees. Toss strawberries with brown sugar and vanilla and arrange on a baking sheet. Roast berries for 15 minutes, or until soft. Remove and let cool.

Heat a grill pan over medium heat. Butter each slice of bread with ½ teaspoon of butter and sprinkle each with ½ teaspoon of turbinado sugar. Place 6 slices of bread, sugar side down, onto hot pan. Place two tablespoons of hazelnut spread onto each slice of bread. Divide berries over hazelnut spread. Sprinkle sugar over remaining buttered slices and place over berries sugared side up.

Brown sandwiches for 2–3 minutes per side, watching carefully so sugar does not burn. Remove sandwiches from heat. Halve each sandwich and serve.

# caramel apple brownie sandwiches

*Caramel apples scream fall. But don't wait until the season strikes to enjoy these sweet treats!*

Prep time: 10 minutes | Cook time: 35 minutes | Makes: 6–8 Sandwiches

BROWNIE

⅔ cup butter, melted
1½ cups brown sugar
2 large eggs
1 teaspoon vanilla
2 cups flour
1 teaspoon baking soda
1 teaspoon salt

APPLES

3 tablespoons butter
1 large green apple, chopped into bite-size chunks
¾ teaspoon cinnamon
½ teaspoon nutmeg
¾ cup brown sugar
½ teaspoon vanilla
⅓ cup evaporated milk

Preheat oven to 350 degrees. Spray a jelly 11 × 17–inch pan.

Melt butter in a bowl. Stir in sugar, eggs, and vanilla extract.

In a separate bowl, combine flour, baking soda, and salt. Add dry ingredients to wet ingredients, stirring just until combined. Pour batter into prepared pan (batter will be thick). Bake brownies for 15–17 minutes or until edges begin to pull away. Do not overbake. Let brownie cool completely.

Heat 3 tablespoons of butter in a small skillet over medium-low heat. Add apples, cinnamon, nutmeg, and brown sugar. Cook for 8–10 minutes, or until soft and tender. Remove from heat and stir in vanilla. Return apples to heat, stir in evaporated milk, and continue to cook 5–8 minutes or until thick and caramelized.

Cut brownies into circles using a 3-inch biscuit cutter. Divide apple mixture among half the circles. Top with remaining circles and serve.

# lemon curd pound cake sandwiches

*Tart lemon curd and sweet raspberry jam make a most merry filling for these simple pound cake sandwiches.*

Prep time: 5 minutes | Cook time: 6 minutes | Makes: 6 sandwiches

- 1 (10.75-oz.) frozen pound cake, thawed, sliced into 12 slices
- 6 teaspoons jarred or homemade lemon curd
- 3 teaspoons raspberry jam

Spray a grill pan with nonstick spray. Place six slices of pound cake down onto hot pan. Top each slice of bread with a teaspoon of lemon curd and a half teaspoon jam. Spray remaining slices and place on sandwich, sprayed side up.

Cook on first side for 2–3 minutes or until golden before heating second side.

# tropical pineapple quesadillas

*Quesadillas for dessert? You bet! The pineapple in these quesadillas sweetens as it heats. The toasted coconut and the macadamia nuts provide the perfect balance.*

Prep time: 5 minutes | Cook time: 6 minutes | Makes: 4 quesadillas

- 1 cup whipping cream
- ¼ cup coconut cream (found in the drink aisle for piña coladas)
- 3 tablespoons powdered sugar
- 4 large tortillas (burrito size)
- 1 pineapple, peeled and sliced into 8 rings
- 1 cup chopped macadamia nuts
- 4 tablespoons caramel sauce
- 1 cup toasted coconut*

Prepare the whipped cream in a chilled bowl by beating heavy whipping cream and coconut cream until it begins to thicken. Sprinkle in powdered sugar 1 tablespoon at a time until stiff peaks form. Refrigerate until ready to serve.

Heat a large skillet over medium heat and spray with nonstick spray. Place one tortilla on the skillet. Slice each pineapple ring in half and place 4 ring halves over one side of the tortilla. Sprinkle pineapple with ¼ cup chopped macadamia nuts and drizzle with 1 tablespoon of caramel sauce. Fold over tortilla.

Cook quesadilla for 2–3 minutes, or until golden brown. Carefully flip quesadilla and brown the second side. Repeat with remaining tortillas and pineapple.

Cut each quesadilla into 3 triangles. Serve with whipped cream and toasted coconut.

*To toast coconut, preheat oven to 325 degrees. Arrange coconut in one layer over a baking sheet. Bake for 15–20 minutes, or until coconut is golden, stirring every 5 minutes.

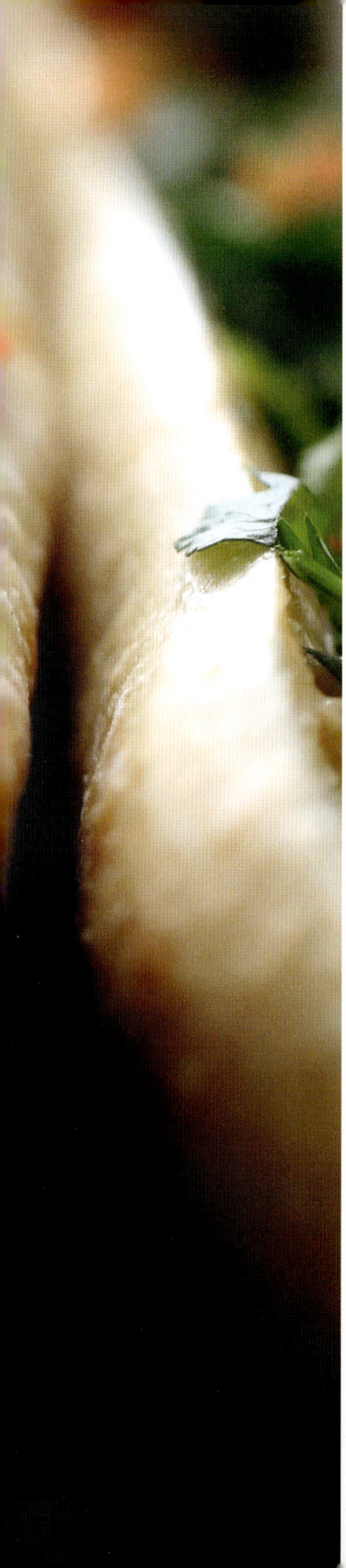

# acknowledgments

I never imagined I'd write a cookbook. If it weren't for my family, it may never have happened. I found the confidence to complete this book because of their unwavering faith and support. The fact that they were willing to eat sandwiches night after night was a bonus!

Thank you to my husband. We go together like peas and carrots. Without you, life would have no flavor. Thank you and your belly for faithfully eating everything I serve day in and day out. No cook could ask for a better taste tester!

Thanks to my kids. You never once complained about all the sandwiches. I'm proud to be your mom and want you to know that this book is all for you. I hope you go through life savoring every morsel! Eat up life as you go along, kids; it's full of sweetness and spice. I love you all, and I love your discerning tastes. You make me a better mom and a better cook.

Thanks to my sisters. Your support has meant everything! How lucky am I to have two enthusiastic cheerleaders in my corner. I'll bring sandwiches to the next happy hour!

Thanks to my mom and dad. Mom, you have shown me that nothing beats homemade food. All the time I spent playing with scraps of dough and licking the bowl as a kid has paid off. Dad, thanks for showing me that in order to grow, you have to take risks.

Thanks to my friends for all your excitement. Testing recipes and taking leftovers was no small task!

Finally, thank you, *Lemon for Lulu* readers, for making this all possible! Thank you for letting me into your kitchens and your lives. Thank you for reading, trying my recipes, and following along. I have the world's best job. I actually get to cook, photograph, and write for a living. If I'm dreaming, please don't wake me. It's just too good.

# Index

## T



## V

# cooking measurement equivalents

| Cups | Tablespoons | Fluid Ounces |
|---|---|---|
| ⅛ cup | 2 Tbsp. | 1 fl. oz. |
| ¼ cup | 4 Tbsp. | 2 fl. oz. |
| ⅓ cup | 5 Tbsp. + 1 tsp. | |
| ½ cup | 8 Tbsp. | 4 fl. oz. |
| ⅔ cup | 10 Tbsp. + 2 tsp. | |
| ¾ cup | 12 Tbsp. | 6 fl. oz. |
| 1 cup | 16 Tbsp. | 8 fl. oz. |

| Cups | Fluid Ounces | Pints/Quarts/Gallons |
|---|---|---|
| 1 cup | 8 fl. oz. | ½ pint |
| 2 cups | 16 fl. oz. | 1 pint = ½ quart |
| 3 cups | 24 fl. oz. | 1½ pints |
| 4 cups | 32 fl. oz. | 2 pints = 1 quart |
| 8 cups | 64 fl. oz. | 2 quarts = ½ gallon |
| 16 cups | 128 fl. oz. | 4 quarts = 1 gallon |

### Other Helpful Equivalents

| | |
|---|---|
| 1 Tbsp. | 3 tsp. |
| 8 oz. | ½ lb. |
| 16 oz. | 1 lb. |

# metric measurement equivalents

## Approximate Weight Equivalents

| Ounces | Pounds | Grams |
|---|---|---|
| 4 oz. | ¼ lb. | 113 g |
| 5 oz. | | 142 g |
| 6 oz. | | 170 g |
| 8 oz. | ½ lb. | 227 g |
| 9 oz. | | 255 g |
| 12 oz. | ¾ lb. | 340 g |
| 16 oz. | 1 lb. | 454 g |

## Approximate Volume Equivalents

| Cups | US Fluid Ounces | Milliliters |
|---|---|---|
| ⅛ cup | 1 fl. oz. | 30 ml |
| ¼ cup | 2 fl. oz. | 59 ml |
| ½ cup | 4 fl. oz. | 118 ml |
| ¾ cup | 6 fl. oz. | 177 ml |
| 1 cup | 8 fl. oz. | 237 ml |

## Other Helpful Equivalents

| | |
|---|---|
| ½ tsp. | 2½ ml |
| 1 tsp. | 5 ml |
| 1 Tbsp. | 15 ml |

# notes

# about the author

Tanya is a wife, a mom to three, a dog lover, a self-taught cook, and a food blogger at *Lemons for Lulu*, where she shares family-friendly recipes that get folks to the table quickly.

Tanya grew up in a Greek household where food often took center stage. She has fond memories of watching her mom cook food "from the old country." Tanya quickly learned that "a pinch of this" and "a little of that" was a way of life. Tanya grew up with a strong appreciation for homemade food, which spills over into the recipes she shares on her blog.

Tanya started *Lemons for Lulu* in 2012 as a way to share her experiments in the kitchen with others. She feels fortunate to be able to share her passion for food and her love of writing in one place.

*Lemons for Lulu* has been featured in *Country Living*, *Parade*, *Cooking Light,* and Buzzfeed. Tanya loves to hear from her readers and welcomes you to her virtual table any time!

0 26575 16973 7